Pare Teacher/Student, Doctor/Patient
New and Selected Poems

Robert H. Deluty

Ben Yehuda Press
Teaneck, New Jersey

PARENT/CHILD, TEACHER/STUDENT, DOCTOR/PATIENT ©2023 Robert H. Deluty. All rights reserved. No part of this book may be used or reproduced in any manner whatsoever without written permission except in the case of brief quotations embodied in critical articles and reviews.

Published by Ben Yehuda Press
122 Ayers Court #1B
Teaneck, NJ 07666

http://www.BenYehudaPress.com

To subscribe to our monthly book club and support independent Jewish publishing, visit https://www.patreon.com/BenYehudaPress

Jewish Poetry Project #34   http://jpoetry.us

Ben Yehuda Press books may be purchased at a discount by synagogues, book clubs, and other institutions buying in bulk. For information, please email markets@BenYehudaPress.com

Library of Congress Cataloging-in-Publication Data

ISBN13 978-1-953829-54-2

23 24 25 / 10 9 8 7 6 5 4 3 2 1   20231005

To

*David,
Laura and Justin,
Ava, Claire, and Diana*

Contents

Euphemisms	1
Live (Long) and Learn	2
Alone	3
Senryu	4
Saturdays	5
Senryu	6
Better than Prozac	7
Special Delivery from Korea	8
In the Community of Scholars	9
Survivor	10
Encores	11
With her Therapist	12
Senryu	13
Alternate Conclusions	14
Birth Father, Birth Mother	15
Laura, at 6	16
At the Market	17
Age/Gender/Temperament	18
Best Defense	19
Halloween at Children's Hospital	20
Jobs	21
Senryu	22
Senryu	23
Senryu	24
One Morning in Academia	25
Senryu	26
Senryu	27
Post-Colloquium	28
Phallic Stage Follies	29
Senryu	30
Retro	31
Senryu	32
Music/Geometry Class	33
Senryu	34

A Minor Shift	35
Senryu	36
Senryu	37
Senryu	38
The Good Fortune of Others	39
Senryu	40
Senryu	41
Senryu	42
Three-Year-Old	43
Freshman	44
The New Member	45
Senryu	46
Senryu	47
Senryu	48
Senryu	49
Senryu	50
First Halloween	51
Senryu	52
For the Record	53
Rest Stop	54
Ivy League	55
Lionhearted	56
Senryu	57
Senryu	58
Thinking Ahead	59
Senryu	60
Any Given Day	61
Senryu	62
Senryu	63
Family Update	64
Breaking the News	65
Brothers	66
About the author	67

Euphemisms

More than the late morning school bus send-offs,
And the parent-friendly homework assignments,
And even the wonderfully awful band recitals,
I will miss his teachers' disciplinary notes,
So artfully phrased and painstakingly inoffensive:

"David had much difficulty today controlling his enthusiasm."
"David is very anxious to share his insights with his neighbors."
"David never misses the opportunity to find humor in seemingly serious situations."

The eleven-year-old class clown,
Graduating to middle school,
Should be thankful for teachers who
Should have been diplomats.

Live (Long) and Learn

Examining the list of support groups
Offered at the retirement community
She is considering, the octogenarian
Pooh-poohs the groups dealing with
Arthritis, osteoporosis, depression,
Parkinson's disease, diabetes,
Chemotherapy, breathing problems,
Anxiety, and macular degeneration,
But shouts *Yes!* upon spotting the title
How to manage your adult children

Alone

As a child in the city
He would dream:
Coming home from school,
All apartment houses on his block
Became precisely the same –
No numbers on buildings,
No letters on doors,
No names on mailboxes.
He couldn't remember
What floor he lived on.
To find his parents,
Every door in every building
Had to be knocked,
Every occupant, disturbed.
He would awaken
Before finding his home,
Crying, terrified.

Thirty years later,
The dream returns –
Not in his sleep,
But when he enters
His child's bedroom
To hold and comfort
In the middle of the night.

Senryu

Professor Bernstein
teaching his Chinese post-doc
Yiddish proverbs

Professor Levine
teaching her Thai grad student
how to make kreplach

their six-year-old,
with a stale French bread,
reinvents baseball

side-by-side, carpooled
eighth grade boys, ninth grade women
sit miles, years apart

at the library
her child searches under "C"
for coloring books

Saturdays

He, raised Orthodox,
Loved the teachings,
Ambivalent about the practice.
His wife, raised agnostic,
Attracted to the fellowship,
Bewildered by the rituals.
Their sons, 7 and 5,
Wanting to spend the morning
In T-shirts, jeans, sneakers.
The family compromise:
Sabbath services at
The Public Library.

Senryu

Jewish vegan's Mom
trying hard to convince him
chicken broth's allowed

Hebrew School class . . .
a first grader asks if God
ever goofs around

a teen's parents
resisting his suggestion
to embrace chaos

a new Ph.D.
insisting his physician
call him *Doctor*

centenarian
preparing noodle kugel
for her senile son

Better than Prozac

A workday's depression
Evaporates as he sees
His child's handiwork in
The backseat of his car:
Gumby, with legs crossed,
Arms outstretched, seat-belted.

Special Delivery from Korea

Airport as maternity hospital.
Arrival gate as waiting room.
Pilot, social worker: midwives.
Baby, conceived and born
Half-a-world away, comes home
To anxious, joyous
Adoptive parents.

In the Community of Scholars

Where shall we eat?
-How about Italian?
No, I'm tired of that. Is anyone up for Thai?
-Too spicy for me. Shall we go with Ruby Tuesday?
Not again! What about that new Korean place?

The dissertation committee
Continues to question and
Deliberate as the Ph.D. student
Paces outside, worrying whether
She has passed her defense.

Survivor

By his own hand, dead at 45.
For decades, his skeleton has
Rattled in the hearts of two daughters.
The younger, now an adult,
Looks at her children, husband.
Terrified of a repetition, she
Curses genetic predispositions,
Wages war against depression,
Vows to celebrate
Her 46th birthday.

Encores

The golden hits of long-forgotten tapes --
"I'll give you something to cry about!"
"Why are you doing this to me?!"
"This is your very last warning!" --
Are reflexively retrieved
As her children repeat
Her own classic routines

Parent/Child, Teacher/Student, Doctor/Patient

With her Therapist

She'll curse, rage, weep. Share
Intimate memories, fears, fantasies.
Reveal dark, petty, infantile shades.
But she won't bare all without
Earrings, lipstick, contact lenses.

Senryu

their daughter Kitty
cautiously begins to date
a man named Katz

thesis defense eve . . .
a grad student fields questions
from her twin toddlers

post Bar Mitzvah,
asking permission to cut
his own bread crusts

Times crossword puzzle . . .
her six-year-old fills each box
with a tiny heart

young psychiatrist
trying in vain to ignore
his patient's beauty

Alternate Conclusions

Grinning from ear to ear,
fifth grade English teacher
Christine Katherine Prine
informs her students that –
as clearly demonstrated by
fettuccine, sine qua non, and
her first, middle, and last names –
the word-ending *ine* can be
pronounced five different ways

Birth Father, Birth Mother

She never asks about him.
It's always her –
How old was she?
What did she look like?
Why did she give me up?
Did she ever hold me?
His absence barely registers.
Hers continues to puzzle
And wound.

Laura, at 6

On the school bus
A third grade boy told me
I have really nice hair.
And Jake, you know, in class,
Said I have a pretty voice.
These,
Her first schoolboy compliments,
Are shared with her parents in
A heartbreaking amalgam of
Pleasure and embarrassment,
Fear and pride.

At the Market

Her five-year-old, deprived of candy,
Pitches a fit. Her four-year-old,
Similarly impoverished,
Throws a tantrum even grander.
Patrons and staff stare,
Shaking their heads in judgment.
Mom looks at children and audience,
Calmly says, "This is the last time
I baby-sit my neighbor's kids."

Age/Gender/Temperament

The emergency room doctor
Concludes it's pneumonia,
So she goes home alone
To pack him a bag and
Inform their children.
She enters the house
Armed with pastries.
The 7-year-old girl
Immediately, fearfully asks
Where's Daddy?
Mom, matter-of-factly,
Lays out the sweets, responds
He needs to stay a few days . . .
Daughter interrupts,
Sobbing hysterically.
Three-year-old son
Ponders it all quietly, asks
Can I have another doughnut?

Best Defense

With twins, parents can
Play kids *man-to-man;*
But, with four, they moan
And must switch to *zone.*

Halloween at Children's Hospital

On the psychiatric wards, it was
More joyous than Christmas,
More treasured than birthdays.
Cookies, candy corn, cupcakes,
Masks, black crepe, skeletons.
A chance to be someone/something else:
The incest victim, a pampered princess;
The frightened boy, a bloodthirsty ghoul;
The psychotic girl, a quiet lake.
A time for receiving without guilt,
For converting true horrors
Into imagined, festive ones.

Jobs

Over the summer, lost
Her Dad to sarcoma.
First day of sixth grade,
Handed a form asking
About her parents' occupations.
Next to Mother, she writes *Nurse*.
Next to Father, *Watching over me.*

Senryu

their child inquiring
how to look hot and be cool
at the same time

the heart surgeon
persuading Saul Bernstein
to get the pig valve

expressing concern
about her therapist's set
of Elvis portraits

Passover morning...
his young son putting matzo
in the toaster

Rose Cohen asking
her forty-year-old gay son
if it's a phase

Senryu

all-star linebacker . . .
his folks remembering him
as a preemie

a chocolatier
describing her parents
as *soft-centered*

dichotomizing
the staff psychiatrists as
med folks or *talkers*

dichotomizing
the staff psychologists as
actives or *passives*

assured by their folks,
when vacationing in Paris,
all foods are kosher

Senryu

the cantor's son
winning the spelling bee
with *Episcopal*

a kindly dentist
dreams of horrified children
fleeing his office

four star restaurant...
spotting a grad student
on financial aid

medical form...
asked her weight, Mom writing
Ten pounds too much

Nobel laureate
thanking his immigrant Dad
for reading to him

One Morning in Academia

The physics professor –
A renowned scholar, writer,
Teacher and mentor –
Stands speechless,
Attempting to formulate
A helpful response to
The student who asked
Why, on every examination,
He only gave credit
For correct answers

Senryu

interfaith household . . .
stuffing their sons' stockings
with Chanukah gelt

hockey star holding
his one-year-old daughter . . .
ten teeth between them

unaware student
plagiarizing an essay
by his professor

waiting in the shop
for his daughter's manicure,
a trucker reads *Vogue*

two narcissists
naming their first child
Mimi

Senryu

orientation . . .
an incoming freshman sleeps
as his Mom takes notes

asking the patient
with the chicken fetish:
Plucked or unplucked?

a one-year-old
using his Dad's violin
as a maraca

to Rorschach Card I
her new patient responding
Lubbock, Texas

to Rorschach Card IV
his new patient responding
Grandpa pole dancing

Post-Colloquium

After observing
His best graduate student
Listen raptly and take
Abundant, meticulous notes
As the eminent scholar
Presented and dissected
His groundbreaking research
For nearly two hours,
He asks the student
Her impressions,
To which she replies
What a hunk!

Phallic Stage Follies

At four,
Legos are shaped into guns,
Popsicle sticks into swords,
Twigs into rifles.
Last night,
Holding a hand-made weapon,
Growls at his father,
"Say yaw pwayyuhs!"
Son, dead serious, views
Himself as Clint Eastwood.
Father, hysterical, sees
A pint-sized Elmer Fudd.

Senryu

asked how he's doing,
her former C+ student
replies *Filthy rich!*

telling her son
to accept on faith
women are wiser

on the internet
trying to locate a mute
for his child's flute

TAs offering
to purchase a *Whack-A-Mole*
for their stressed prof

a grieving Dad
wondering if babies age
in heaven

Retro

Upon returning home
From a visit to Grandma,
His daughter requests
For her ninth birthday
A manual typewriter:
It's the coolest thing, Dad.
A word processor and printer
All in one!

Senryu

Israel's leader? . . .
a tenth grader writing
Nathan Yahoo

a Baptist girl
asking her Jewish teacher
Am I a goy?

a college senior
requesting that his shrink
adopt him

spring break . . .
their sixth grader creating
a new alphabet

dinner with Mom . . .
an OCD man bringing
his own silverware

Music/Geometry Class

Lacking the bongos,
Timpani, tom-toms,
Congas and tambourines
To create a drum circle,
Four kindergartners
Take their instruments,
Spread apart and form
A triangle square

Senryu

the rabbi's son
naming his tropical fish
Gefilte

unemployed artist
watching an in-flight movie
starring his mother

nutrition class . . .
a student asks if beer nuts
are legumes

her teen's eyes roll
as she stoops to pick up
a curbside nickel

post eye surgery . . .
a patient tells her doctor
to trim his sideburns

A Minor Shift

Spotting on the same page
in her pocket dictionary,
the negatively connoted words
sneak, sneer, snide, snigger,
snipe, snippy, snivel, snob,
snooty, snort and snot,
nine-year-old Rebecca
asks her parents if they can
change their last name from
Snell to Shell

Senryu

playing with his son,
jotting down a haiku spark
in crayon

on the boardwalk
a Mom pushing her four kids
in a shopping cart

genetics class . . .
the teacher is asked whether
bad luck is passed down

a grad student
proposing for his thesis
Women & Their Shoes

a paranoid man
firing his psychologist
for asking questions

Senryu

an author's mother
stealing the hubcaps
of a critic's car

first night out...
new parents talking about
the baby's stool

a failing student
arguing that his teacher
has no right to judge

pre-surgery,
studying her doctor's hand...
one dirty nail

correcting his son:
Uncle Sol is a shlemiel,
not a nudnik

Senryu

under fire, ruing
the decision to enlist
to please his Dad

a frozen PC . . .
two professors summoning
their third grader

informing her child
that there are love taps
but not love chokes

twenty years later
sending his fifth grade teacher
a thank-you note

two musicians
learning their newborn
is stone deaf

The Good Fortune of Others

Friday morning, late May.
A colleague relates
How exhausted she is after
Attending four nights in a row
Award banquets
For her high school senior,
A superb scholar, artist, musician
And athlete.

He reflects on his own senior --
   On his skipping classes,
   On his stints in detention,
   On his recent suspension,
   On his overall G.P.A. of 2.15 --
And resists a powerful urge
To beat the colleague senseless.

Senryu

suspicions mount . . .
their three sons volunteering
to clean the garage

a fourth grade poet
asking his father to rhyme
gladiola

three inpatients
rating their psychiatrists
on sex appeal

You're doubly blessed . . .
exhausted mother of twins
offers no response

telling the teacher
to ignore him if his hand
is not raised

Senryu

on Passover . . .
father and son discussing
God and macaroons

sex ed student
asking if any countries
prohibit foreplay

longtime patient
demanding an invitation
to her shrink's wedding

the rich man's child
noting she'd like to be poor
for one hour

five-year-old blind girl . . .
her mother tries to describe
the evening's rainbow

Senryu

doctor's office wall...
underneath the diplomas
his baby's footprints

describing his folks
as perpetually broke,
yet never poor

old psychiatrist
in a downtown porn shop
claiming it's research

after the car wash
drying off his young daughter
with a leaf blower

on death row, musing
how he would have turned out
with loving parents

Three-Year-Old

Daughter of two psychologists,
Witnesses them arguing.
Screams at each,
"What's your issue?!"
Her parents, terrified,
Anticipate adolescence.

Freshman

Came for advisement.
Missing six fingers,
Three from each hand.
Left wrist bore a grid of
Short, razor-thin scars.
Eyes, unable to make contact,
Danced wildly about the room.
Fragile, frightened, damaged,
Appeared a victim of abuse
(Both self- and other-inflicted).
First words:
Tell me what to take,
I want to help people.

The New Member

Staring at their baby sister
They worry.
Aged 8 and 5.
Adopted as infants.
They understand that the baby
Is their parents' only birth child.
The eldest verbalizes the fear:
Mom and Dad won't love her as much.
She wasn't chosen like we were.

Senryu

next morning . . .
the bride's Dad finding rice
in his wallet

telling the doctor
why empty calories
are her favorites

dentist's office . . .
an old man asks the price
of cleaning three teeth

Yeshiva student
questioning his teacher
about porkpie hats

grocery checkout . . .
standing beside the teacher
whose class he cut

Senryu

perfectionist
worrying she'll disappoint
her psychiatrist

baby boomer's son
finds a mauve Nehru jacket
in his Dad's closet

visiting hours . . .
their schizophrenic daughter
blaming them and God

renowned therapist,
lauded by strangers world-wide,
feeling lost at home

teacher with cancer
listening to her students
whine about finals

Senryu

NA meeting . . .
their twelve-year-old admits
she's an addict

fourth grade teacher
explains why effort alone
deserves no *A*

absent student
e-mailing her professor,
Send me your notes :-)

old French professor,
young Haitian janitor
swapping idioms

their aged father
escaping depression
via dementia

Senryu

first day of school . . .
wiping away the tears
of her husband

reading Tolstoy
as her child completes mile eight
of a marathon

parents pondering
where to draw the line between
quirky and *scary*

two young mothers
comparing the talents
of their newborns

highly anxious girl,
unorthodox therapist
meeting at IHOP

Senryu

dirt-filled popgun
discharges in a child's eyes . . .
Dad licking them clean

before the spanking,
a boy stuffing marshmallows
in his back pockets

their preschooler,
attempting to stop time,
unplugs the clock

warning her son
that rolling one's eyes
causes blindness

bewildered children
don't recognize the parent
being eulogized

First Halloween

Aged two, dressed as a Dalmatian,
He knocks and rings, and
When doors open, marches
Directly into strangers' kitchens
Looking for treasures.

Late in the evening, he
Spies a cat and madly takes off.
Poor bewildered feline –
Being chased by a 2-legged dog
In turn pursued by an exhausted
Father with a flashlight.

Senryu

three-year-old's ear ...
ER doctor performing
a raisinectomy

a vice principal
chiding the teacher who hugged
a distraught student

Econ I midterm ...
overhearing a freshman
talking in his sleep

quintuplets born
February twenty-ninth ...
Dad ponders the odds

summer school teacher
pelted with trash for saying
We're gonna have fun!

For the Record

New next-door neighbors
James and Mary Smith –
After introducing their sons
Al, Ed, Ben, and Lew –
Make a point of noting
The boys' given names are
Aloysius, Edmund,
Bentley and Llewellyn

Rest Stop

New Jersey Turnpike men's room.
Three-year-old boy drops his pants,
Walks over to the children's urinal
And goes to work.
To his right stand
Six leather-and-chain clad
Motorcyclists, similarly engaged.
Father of the boy observes
The magnificent seven from behind
And longs for a camera.

Ivy League

Seven minutes before
The scheduled start of the final,
The instructor for the
Introduction to Psychology class
Of two hundred, twenty-four pupils
Receives an e-mail from
An honors student inquiring
Where will the exam be held

Lionhearted

Amidst a forest of legs –
Table, chair, and human –
The intrepid toddler lurches,
Caroming off hard bodies
Like a multi-limbed pinball.
Falling, rising, falling, rising.
A courageous, undaunted explorer
Seeking adventure and knowledge
In a land of giants.

Senryu

wallet-sized photo . . .
his depressed adult daughter
as a smiling child

their six-year-old
asking the flight attendant
for a milkshake

down-and-out parents
saving Halloween candy
for Thanksgiving

odd-numbered candles,
even-numbered children . . .
Chanukah fractions

at the bus stop
her second grader's new shoes
find an old puddle

Senryu

Independence Day . . .
covering her toddler's ears,
she stares skyward

young music student
asking which instrument
attracts the most girls

psychotherapist
at breakfast, analyzing
his daughter's dream

before surgery
a young cancer patient
calming her mother

abused child
surprised by the fear
in his father's eyes

Thinking Ahead

The elderly professor –
Observing in his class
The faux hawks, ear spacers,
Argyles with sandals, pajamas,
Crocs clogs, sagging pants,
Whole arm, leg, and back tattoos,
Ripped jeans, backward baseball caps,
Together with lip, tongue, chin, forehead,
Cheek, eyebrow, and septum piercings –
Tries to envision his students'
Future employers and children

Senryu

doctor's waiting room . . .
three pregnant adolescents
doing their homework

blushing physician . . .
half-naked female patient
knows his mother

their child in shul . . .
his eyes closed, praying
for the sermon to end

laundry day . . .
Mom finding Brussel sprouts
stuffed in each napkin

their daughter's prom date . . .
his purple hair complements
her pink corsage

Any Given Day

demon/angel, taker/giver, lion/lamb,
goddess/monster, outsider/insider,
believer/heretic, thanker/ingrate, child/adult,
utopian/nihilist, comedienne/tragedienne,
genius/ignoramus, ogre/enchantress, teenager

Senryu

mother of five
purchasing diapers
for her parents

astronomy class . . .
bracing for wisecracks,
he says *Uranus*

a grandfather cries
hearing his son called *Papa*
for the first time

senior prom night . . .
strapless gown on her bed
next to teddy bears

Christmas tradition . . .
Jewish family dining
with chopsticks

Senryu

hyperactive child
in Grand Central Station
blending unnoticed

roadside diner . . .
their five-year-old downing
shots of half-and-half

Rabbi Feldman
depicting Adam as
the #1 Dad

sixth grade teacher
noting *comes to fruition*
does not mean *ripen*

telling his children
if nobody hates you,
you're unworthy

Family Update

Asked about his adult children,
Judge Irwin Shapiro replies
My older daughter is a diplomat
living in Marseilles;
My younger daughter is a surgeon
living in San Francisco; and
My son is chronically unemployed
and living on my couch.

Breaking the News

After several weeks of
Contemplation and rehearsal,
She approaches with fear and sadness
Rachel, her fourteen-year-old daughter,
And announces that
She and Rachel's stepfather
Are divorcing.

Rachel, visibly shocked,
Stares at her mother,
Begins to sob, and utters softly,
Birthday wishes do come true.

Brothers

Mom died, and they came
To divide the estate.
A coin flip would determine
Who chose first.
Knowing his brother as he did,
Knowing his love of family,
Of music, of tradition,
The younger knew the elder would select
The portrait of their father cradling
His cherished violin.

The coin was tossed, the younger won.
The portrait! The portrait!, he cried.
Thank goodness, sighed the elder.
I was afraid you'd select
The big screen television.

About the author

Dr. Robert H. Deluty is Associate Dean Emeritus of the Graduate School at the University of Maryland, Baltimore County. A psychology professor at UMBC from 1980 to 2016, he was named Presidential Teaching Professor in 2002. Dr. Deluty's poems and essays have been published in *The Wall Street Journal, The Baltimore Sun, The Pegasus Review, Modern Haiku, Voices: The Art and Science of Psychotherapy, Psychiatric Times, Jewish Currents,* the *Journal of Poetry Therapy, Welcome Home, Muse of Fire, Maryland Family Magazine, Gastronomica: The Journal of Food and Culture, The Faculty Voice,* and many other newspapers, journals, and anthologies. *Parent/Child, Teacher/Student, Doctor/Patient* is his sixty-sixth book.

The Jewish Poetry Project

jpoetry.us

Ben Yehuda Press

From the Coffee House of Jewish Dreamers: Poems of Wonder and Wandering and the Weekly Torah Portion by Isidore Century

"Isidore Century is a wonderful poet. His poems are funny, deeply observed, without pretension." – *The Jewish Week*

The House at the Center of the World: Poetic Midrash on Sacred Space by Abe Mezrich

"Direct and accessible, Mezrich's midrashic poems often tease profound meaning out of his chosen Torah texts. These poems remind us that our Creator is forgiving, that the spiritual and physical can inform one another, and that the supernatural can be carried into the everyday."
—Yehoshua November, author of *God's Optimism*

we who desire: Poems and Torah riffs by Sue Swartz

"Sue Swartz does magnificent acrobatics with the Torah. She takes the English that's become staid and boring, and adds something that's new and strange and exciting. These are poems that leave a taste in your mouth, and you walk away from them thinking, what did I just read? Oh, yeah. It's the Bible."
—Matthue Roth, author of *Yom Kippur A Go-Go*

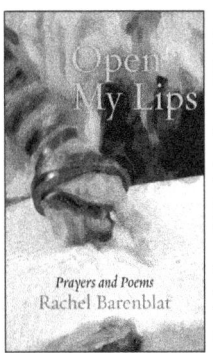

Open My Lips: Prayers and Poems by Rachel Barenblat

"Barenblat's God is a personal God—one who lets her cry on His shoulder, and who rocks her like a colicky baby. These poems bridge the gap between the ineffable and the human. This collection will bring comfort to those with a religion of their own, as well as those seeking a relationship with some kind of higher power."
—Satya Robyn, author of *The Most Beautiful Thing*

Words for Blessing the World: Poems in Hebrew and English by Herbert J. Levine

"These writings express a profoundly earth-based theology in a language that is clear and comprehensible. These are works to study and learn from."
—Rodger Kamenetz, author of *The Jew in the Lotus*

Shiva Moon: Poems by Maxine Silverman

"The poems, deeply felt, are spare, spoken in a quiet but compelling voice, as if we were listening in to her inner life. This book is a precious record of the transformation saying Kaddish can bring."
—Howard Schwartz, author of *The Library of Dreams*

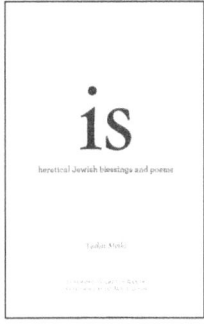

is: heretical Jewish blessings and poems by Yaakov Moshe (Jay Michaelson)

"Finally, Torah that speaks to and through the lives we are actually living: expanding the tent of holiness to embrace what has been cast out, elevating what has been kept down, advancing what has been held back, reveling in questions, revealing contradictions."
—Eden Pearlstein, aka eprhyme

Texts to the Holy: Poems
by Rachel Barenblat

"These poems are remarkable, radiating a love of God that is full bodied, innocent, raw, pulsating, hot, drunk. I can hardly fathom their faith but am grateful for the vistas they open. I will sit with them, and invite you to do the same."
—Merle Feld, author of *A Spiritual Life*

The Sabbath Bee: Love Songs to Shabbat
by Wilhelmina Gottschalk

"Torah, say our sages, has seventy faces. As these prose poems reveal, so too does Shabbat. Here we meet Shabbat as familiar housemate, as the child whose presence transforms a family, as a spreading tree, as an annoying friend who insists on being celebrated, as a woman, as a man, as a bee, as the ocean."
—Rachel Barenblat, author of *The Velveteen Rabbi's Haggadah*

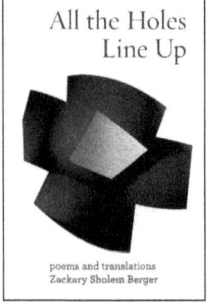

All the Holes Line Up: Poems and Translations
by Zackary Sholem Berger

"Spare and precise, Berger's poems gaze unflinchingly at—but also celebrate—human imperfection in its many forms. And what a delight that Berger also includes in this collection a handful of his resonant translations of some of the great Yiddish poets." —Yehoshua November, author of *God's Optimism* and *Two World Exist*

How to Bless the New Moon:
Songs of the Sovereign and the Icon
by Rachel Kann

"Rachel Kann is a master wordsmith. Her poems are rich in content, packed with life's wisdom and imbued with soul. May this collection of her work enable more of the world to enjoy her offerings."
—Sarah Yehudit Schneider, author of *You Are What You Hate* and *Kabbalistic Writings on the Nature of Masculine and Feminine*

Into My Garden
by David Caplan

"The beauty of Caplan's book is that it is not polemical. It does not set out to win an argument or ask you whether you've put your tefillin on today. These gentle poems invite the reader into one person's profound, ambiguous religious experience."
—*The Jewish Review of Books*

Between the Mountain and the Land is the Lesson: Poetic Midrash on Sacred Community
by Abe Mezrich

"Abe Mezrich cuts straight back to the roots of the Midrashic tradition, sermonizing as a poet, rather than idealogue. Best of all, Abe knows how to ask questions and avoid the obvious answers."
—Jake Marmer, author of *Jazz Talmud*

NOKADDISH: Poems in the Void
by Hanoch Guy Kaner

"A subversive, midrashic play with meanings—specifically Jewish meanings, and then the reversal and negation of these meanings."
—Robert G. Margolis

An Added Soul: Poems for a New Old Religion
by Herbert J. Levine

"These poems are remarkable, radiating a love of God that is full bodied, innocent, raw, pulsating, hot, drunk. I can hardly fathom their faith but am grateful for the vistas they open. I will sit with them, and invite you to do the same."
—Merle Feld, author of *A Spiritual Life*.

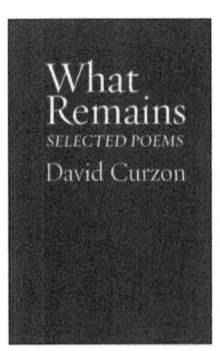

What Remains
by David Curzon

"Aphoristic, ekphrastic, and precise revelations animate WHAT REMAINS. In his stunning rewriting of Psalm 1 and other biblical passages, Curzon shows himself to be a fabricator, a collector, and an heir to the literature, arts, and wisdom traditions of the planet."
—Alicia Ostriker, author of *The Volcano and After*

The Shortest Skirt in Shul
by Sass Oron

"These poems exuberantly explore gender, Torah, the masks we wear, and the way our bodies (and the ways we wear them) at once threaten stable narratives, and offer the kind of liberation that saves our lives."
—Alicia Jo Rabins, author of *Divinity School*, composer of *Girls In Trouble*

Walking Triptychs
by Ilya Gutner

These are poems from when I walked about Shanghai and thought about the meaning of the Holocaust.

Book of Failed Salvation
by Julia Knobloch

"These beautiful poems express a tender longing for spiritual, physical, and emotional connection. They detail a life in movement—across distances, faith, love, and doubt."
—David Caplan, author of *Into My Garden*

Daily Blessings: Poems on Tractate Berakhot
by Hillel Broder

"Hillel Broder does not just write poetry about the Talmud; he also draws out the Talmud's poetry, finding lyricism amidst legality and re-setting the Talmud's rich images like precious gems in end-stopped lines of verse."
—Ilana Kurshan, author of *If All the Seas Were Ink*

The Missing Jew: Poems 1976-2022
by Rodger Kamenetz

"How does Rodger Kamenetz manage to have so singular a voice and at the same time precisely encapsulate the world view of an entire generation (also mine) of text-hungry American Jews born in the middle of the twentieth century?"
—Jacqueline Osherow, author of *Ultimatum from Paradise* and *My Lookalike at the Krishna Temple: Poems*

The Red Door: A dark fairy tale told in poems
by Shawn C. Harris

"THE RED DOOR, like its poet author Shawn C. Harris, transcends genres and identities. It is an exploration in crossing worlds. It brings together poetry and story telling, imagery and life events, spirit and body, the real and the fantastic, Jewish past and Jewish present, to spin one tale."
—Einat Wilf, author of *The War of Return*

The Matter of Families
by Robert H. Deluty

"Robert Deluty's career-spanning collection of New and Selected poems captures the essence of his work: the power of love, joy, and connection, all tied together with the poet's glorious sense of humor. This book is Deluty's masterpiece."
—Richard M. Berlin, M.D., author of *Freud on My Couch*

The Five Books of Limericks
by Rhonda Rosenheck

"A biblical commentary that is truly unique. Each chapter of the Torah is distilled into its own limerick, leading the reader to reconsider the meaning of the original text, and opening avenues for interpretation that are both fun and insightful."
—Rabbi Hillel Norry

Bits and Pieces
by Edward Pomerantz

"A stunning tapestry of family life in the 40s and 50s. Like all great poetry, Pomerantz's work expands after reading. Each poem is exquisitely structured, often with a stunning ending, into a masterful whole."
—Alan Ziegler, editor of SHORT: An International Anthology

Words for a Dazzling Firmament: Poems/Readings on Bereishit Through Shemot
by Abe Mezrich

"Mezrich is a cultivated craftsman— interpretively astute, sonically deliberate, and spiritually cunning."
—Zohar Atkins, author of Nineveh

Everything Thaws
by R. B. Lemberg

"Full of glacier-sharp truths, and moments revealed between words like bodies beneath melting permafrost. As it becomes increasingly plain how deeply our world is shaped by war and climate change and grief and anger, articulating that shape feels urgent and necessary and painful and healing."
—Ruthanna Emrys, author of A Half-Built Garden

Ode to the Dove
An illustrated, bilingual edition of a Yiddish poem by Abraham Sutzkever
Zackary Sholem Berger, translator
Liora Ostroff, Illustrator

"An elegant volume for lovers of poetry."
—Justin Cammy, translator of Sutzkever, *From the Vilna Ghetto to Nuremberg: Memoir and Testimony*

Poems for a Cartoon Mouse
by Andrew Burt

"Andrew Burt's poetry magnifies the vanishingly small line between danger and safety. This collection asks whether order is an illusion that veils chaos, or vice-versa, juxtaposing images from the Bible with animated films."
—Ari Shapiro, host of NPR's *All Things Considered*

Old Shul
by Pinny Bulman

"Nostalgia gives way to a tender theology, a softly chuckling illumination from within the heart of/as a beautiful, broken sanctuary, somehow both gritty and fragile, grimy and iridescent – not unlike faith itself."
—Jake Marmer, author of *Cosmic Diaspora*

Feet In L.A., But My Womb Lives In Jerusalem, My Breath In Vermont
by Lori Levy

"Reading through Lori Levy's new book of poems takes my breath away. With no pretense whatsoever, they leap, alive, from the page until this reader felt as if she were living Levy's life. How does the author do it?"
—Mary Jo Balistreri, author of *Still*

www.ingramcontent.com/pod-product-compliance
Lightning Source LLC
LaVergne TN
LVHW042117070225
803225LV00041B/1167